THE
ART OF
NAPPING

THE
ART OF
NAPPING

WILLIAM A. ANTHONY, PH.D.

PUBLISHED FOR THE PAUL BRUNTON PHILOSOPHIC FOUNDATION BY
LARSON PUBLICATIONS

ON THE COVER: *Sleeping Eros,* bronze, 3nd–2rd century B.C., by permission of The Metropolitan Museum of Art, Rogers Fund, 1943. (43.11.4)

International Standard Book Number: 0-943914-82-5
Library of Congress Catalog Card Number: 97-70331

Published for the Paul Brunton Philosophic Foundation by
Larson Publications
4936 NYS Route 414, Burdett, New York 14818 USA

02 01 00 99 98 97

10 9 8 7 6 5 4 3 2

Publisher and author gratefully acknowledge the following for permission to use material under copyright as epigraphs:
    Chapter 2: Claudio Stampi, *Why We Nap*, Birkhauser, Boston, © 1991. Chapter 3: Reprinted courtesy of Houghton-Mifflen. Chapter 4: Reprinted by permission of *Wall Street Journal*, © 1995 Dow Jones & Company, Inc. All Rights Reserved Worldwide. Chapter 5: Reprinted by permission of the publisher, from HR FOCUS MARCH 1995. American Management Association, New York. All rights reserved. Chapter 7: Reprinted with permission of The Free Press, a division of Simon & Schuster from SLEEP THIEVES: An Eye-opening Exploration Into the Science and Mysteries of Sleep by Stanley Coren. Copyright © 1996 by Stanley Coren.

CONTENTS

ACKNOWLEDGEMENTS AND KUDOS

To my cousin Denny, whose prodigious napping feats helped to stimulate this book;

To my cousin Tom, who for Christmas gave me my first napsack filled with napnomic devices;

To my daughters Julia, Jill, and Jessica, who as kid-nappers gave me someone with whom to nap, and as young women are continuing the family napping tradition;

To my wife Camille, who naps like she does most everything else in her life, with enthusiasm and confidence;

To my mother and father, who like good parents everywhere instilled in me an early appreciation of napping;

To my older brothers Bob, Jack, and Dick, who nurtured my

napping expertise as a way to keep me from bothering them;

To all my other napkin, who make family gatherings a special place and time for guilt-free napping;

To all my friends whom I observed napping at concerts, movies, and on vacations, and whose company often put me to sleep;

To Amy and Paul of Larson Publications, who believe in this book and its topic;

To the staff at the Reading Public Library, where I did both my library and my laboratory research;

To all my napping colleagues around the world who as proud nappers realize that napping can be the no-cost, no-sweat way to physical and emotional health.

z   z   z

THE ART OF NAPPING

*Why do I have to take a nap?
I'm not tired.*
—Scarlett O'Hara in
Gone With the Wind

AN INTRODUCTION TO THE WORLD OF NAPPING

Scarlett O'Hara indeed had a lot to learn! The quote above captures the most important piece of information that she lacked. Despite her apparent worldliness she didn't know why she should nap! It's a question that has plagued our society as well. Many people don't know about the benefits of napping—another example of forgetting what we learned as children!

Still other people feel guilty about their napping. They hide the fact that they do nap. They might even obstruct the naps of others—an act tantamount to defying the teachings of their own mothers!

I was once told by a policeman that I could not nap in a public place. Most Nap Police are not in uniform, but they are everywhere, masquerading as civilians, doing what they think is their civic duty: waking nappers, making them ashamed of napping, and all without the least understanding of nap etiquette.

Nappism

We live in a nappist society—where napping is discriminated against. This goes on despite the fact that medical researchers say we're nearly all seriously "sleep-deprived." Unlike Scarlett, most of us are very tired! How much longer can we support nappism's tired clichés?

It is time for napping to come out of the closet and take its rightful place in the living room, the workplace and any place. Napping is bipartisan—it may be the only desirable similarity between presidents Reagan and Clinton. Napping occurs across the age span and around the world. Most mammals nap. Lack of napping behavior is the exception, not the rule. Indeed, a majority of people nap—but they don't talk about it in public. Napping is a natural, normal, and—dare I say— even a Godlike process.

THE ART OF NAPPING

Napping Role Models

As the Bible says, "on the seventh day . . . God rested." *Even God naps!* I suspect that in earlier translations of the Bible the text read that "on the seventh day God nappeth."

And God is not the only famous napper. Brahms napped at the piano while he composed his famous lullaby. Napoleon napped between battles. Churchill maintained that he had to nap in order to cope with his wartime responsibilities. Geniuses such as Edison and Da Vinci napped. Obviously nappers are in good company.

Thank God for nappers. They know how to get more done and have more fun!

Scientists at the Nappers' Bedside

Scientists are discovering the awesome power of napping. The science of napping (or what I call *No-nap-apology*) is providing us with facts about napping. Scientists (no-nap-apologists) who study napping have reported that about sixty percent of adults nap at least once a week. The time of most naps ranges from fifteen minutes to two hours. Scientific studies have shown that naps can have a positive effect on both mood and performance. It is one of those rare instances where science says that something I like is actually good for me!

While some naps help people overcome their tiredness, other naps occur because *people simply like to take naps.* Still other naps are used to prepare people for anticipated late nights. Most nappers know experientially that naps feel good and enhance their physical and emotional functioning. Science is concluding empirically what nappers have known for a long time: **Napping can be good for your health.**

Napping Pride

Yet few people are proud nappers. Most have incorporated the stigma of society into their own napping life. As a result, they can't discuss napping strategies and personal napping highlights with fellow nappers. They remain silent when people make fun of nappers. They pretend they are meditating when in fact they are napping. They can not converse in the language of napping. They do not know the nap histories of famous nappers. They can not attack the myths of napping that have been perpetrated by our nappist society. They are ashamed to brag about their napping. They believe that you "steal a nap" rather than "revel in a nap." Nappers must no longer close their eyes to such behavior. *It is time for nappers to lie down and be counted!*

During the gestation and writing period for *The Art of*

Napping, I have reveled in hundreds of naps. May you as its reader be blessed with many good naps while reading it.

Nap Management

As you become a proud napper, you also can become a more skillful napper. In settings which still discriminate against nappers (such as most work settings) you can learn how to disguise your nap. One can learn napping techniques and strategies that have been successful for others. Do you know the different strategies people use to nap at work? Have you talked about nap strategies with your fellow employees—and how about your boss? Maybe your boss needs a copy of *The Art of Napping*—an anonymous gift perhaps!? *The Art of Napping* can help you become a better manager of your own nap behavior, and be a consultant to other fellow nappers and would-be nappers. Better nap management allows you to plan your next nap while you're taking your current nap. Proud napping portends a future of relaxation.

A Society of Nappers

Our future society will be more supportive of napping. A nap industry will evolve. Harbingers of that industry are already present. People are already conducting nap seminars. Desks with built-in beds for napping are now available. The federal government supports napping research. More and more people will come to realize the direct and indirect benefits of napping. *The Art of Napping* will help prepare you for a non-nappist society. Indeed, you can help bring it about. You may wish to take a nap right now. I think I'm ready for a nap too!

See you on the other side.

z   z   z

THE ART OF NAPPING

The study of a putative polyphasic tendency or capacity of the human sleep system represents a broad physiological interest both for speculative issues related to the function of sleep and for its practical applications for human functioning.

—Claudio Stampi, in *Why We Nap*

NONAPAPOLOGY:
THE SCIENCE OF NAPPING

Wow! It is obvious from the preceding quote that the writings of sleep researchers stimulate many non-scientists to nap! They are "couching" in the language of science what nappers have learned personally on their own couch. Nappers have conducted their own personal research on napping for years, not in the laboratory but in the real world. Nappers and nonapapologists report similar findings. They just use different words.

In the esoteric words of the scientific community, as exemplified in the writings of David Dinges, ". . . napping can often be an attractive option, reflecting a chronobiologically regulated sleep tendency that is amplified by sleep pressure and gated by environmental opportunity." How delightful by contrast is the napper-friendly, simple wording of the napping community: "Naps are natural. They are good for you. Nap whenever you have a chance."

Understanding Nonapapology

Yet the science of nonapapology is important for nappers to know. Science can help destroy myths and overcome prejudices. Nappers can use the facts of nonapapology to help them bring napping into the mainstream. A well-rounded naptivist knows not only his or her personal napping facts, but also the general knowledge of the science of napping.

While it may appear to some nappers that the study of nonapapology is simply researching common sense, we must realize that common sense about napping is not common in many countries. If napping were common sense there would be couches at the symphony, at baseball games, in airports, and everywhere else that people commonly nap. Where wouldn't there be couches, anyway?

Misleading Dictionary Definition

Science often starts with a definition. Webster's dictionary defines nap as "a brief period of sleep." However, even dictionary definitions of nap reveal society's prejudices. Sometimes included in the definition is the phrase "as taken by infants." Nappers would ask why the modifying phrase does not read something like *"as taken by leaders and geniuses."*

THE ART OF NAPPING

In the Eyes of the Beholder

There seems to be no one common definition of nap—which is good, because every napper lives out their own personal definition. Wilse Webb quotes a fictional character who says that a nap is "any rest period up to twenty minutes' duration involving unconsciousness but not pajamas." As we will see later, this definition would exclude the naps of one of the most famous proponents of napping—Winston Churchill.

My most fastidious daughter has an even more pragmatic definition of napping: "sleep when you don't brush your teeth or wash your face beforehand." However that definition would include all sleeping behavior (i.e., naps as well as night-time sleep) of one of my least fastidious nephews.

It seems that no one definition of a nap will suffice. A nap, like beauty, is in the eyes of the beholder, or in this instance, in the somnolent eyes of the napper.

Discrediting Napping Myths

The science of nonapapology has provided nappers with facts to counteract harmful myths about napping which have been perpetrated by napaphobic members of our society. These myths serve to reinforce society's discriminatory practices against nappers. In addition, these myths of napping justify, for some people, their reluctance to become nappers. Once nappers understand that napping myths are simply the tired clichés of equally tired people, nappers will assertively counter these myths with the facts of napping.

Is Liking to Nap a Disorder?

One of the more damaging napping myths is that napping is somehow abnormal. People who nap are made to feel guilty and ashamed. They may incorporate the prejudices of napaphobics and believe themselves to be slothful or malingerers.

In contrast to this myth of abnormality, nonapapology has found that the desire to nap is normal. It is not a reflection of pathology or even an indicator of the presence of sleep problems. Napping is an expression of an underlying biological rhythm, a normal behavior of normal people. What is perhaps abnormal is society's propensity to discourage napping. The work schedules and attitudes toward napping of our nappist society have made the normal appear abnormal!

Is It Possible to Take an After-Lunch Nap without the Lunch?

Another myth is that the desire for a post-lunch nap is due to a need to rest after eating. Or said another way, napping is encouraged by the digestion of the noon-time meal. In contrast

to this myth, Nonapapologists have found that afternoon sleepiness occurs whether or not a meal is eaten. Also, the afternoon period is not the only time when the desire for napping is strong. When people are allowed to nap whenever they like, there appears to be a propensity to nap in the late morning. The afternoon nap is the most popular, however, and it seems to occur about midway between when we wake in the morning and go to sleep at night. For example, someone who is awake sixteen hours a day— from 7 A.M. to 11 P.M.—would be most eager to nap somewhere around 3 P.M.

Is There a Best Time to Nap?

Related to the preceding myth is the myth that there is an ideal nap period and place. Nappers are unique individuals, and each must learn the various times and places that make the most sense to him or her. While the afternoon time between 2 P.M. and 5 P.M. is a very common nap period, late morning naps may also be advantageous. Gifted nappers quickly get in touch with their own napping cycles and rhythms and, as we shall see later, their own napping places.

Does a Nap Interfere with Night-time Sleep?

Here is yet another myth that prevents some would-be nappers from becoming nappers: They incorrectly believe that napping reduces one's ability to sleep at night. The research of nonapapologists has uncovered no proof that naps make it difficult for one to sleep at night. Nappers report no greater night-time sleep difficulties than non-nappers. A good nap and a good night-time sleep can go hand in hand. It sounds like the best of both worlds.

Making the Most of One's Napping Opportunities

Much of the research on napping has been conducted on college students. This should come as no surprise, as they have the flexibility in their schedule to nap and they live in a setting where researchers work.

Another adult group in which naps often occur is the elderly. The question remains as to whether the daytime naps of the elderly are due to some biological reason, or perhaps due to the fact that the elderly have more opportunity to nap!

Nappers would argue that if adults are given the opportunity to nap, no matter what their age, they will nap more frequently. Flight attendants, for example, tell me that a majority of passengers nap. Adults with schedules that permit napping (college students and the elderly) nap more often. And who amongst the napping community would blame them? Napping keeps a lot of people in school, and it's one of the joys of growing old.

Knowing about Sleep Inertia

Of interest to nappers and would-be nappers is the research on "sleep inertia." *Yes, I know it sounds technical but don't nap through this page.* Or if you must so flatter me, then return as soon as possible to try it again—it's important.

Sleep inertia refers to the detrimental effects of napping on performance and mood immediately after awakening from a nap. Almost everyone who has napped has at times experienced an uncomfortable feeling of confusion or disorientation upon awakening from a nap. Sleep inertia is of most concern to novice nappers, who don't understand that this is a normal feeling which disappears quickly. Sleep inertia is often the reason why some people refuse to nap.

The important research finding is that sleep inertia usually disappears in fifteen minutes or less, while improvements in mood and performance may last for hours. In a later chapter on managing your nap, various strategies for overcoming sleep inertia will be mentioned. However, the take-to-your-bed message from the research is that sleep inertia is transient and in no way interferes with the benefits of napping.

Your Three Basic Nap Groups

Nonapologists have identified and labeled three types of napping behavior: *1. replacement napping* (a great way to reward yourself for staying up late kind of nap); *2. prophylactic napping* (nap now so you won't pay for it later kind of nap); and *3. appetitive napping* (if it feels good just do it kind of nap). An expert napper can employ all three types of napping behavior simultaneously if the need exists. (You are tired from last night, you might get tired tonight, and it just feels good anyway kind of nap.) For ease of remembering I have alliterated the three basic napping groups thusly: 1) **preventive,** 2) **preparatory,** and 3) **pleasurable.**

Preventive Napping to Avoid Sleep Deprivation

Most adults are introduced to the world of napping through preventive or replacement napping. The purpose of preventive napping, as the name implies, is to prevent sleep deprivation or to replace lost sleep. Preventive napping is designed to overcome a previous lack of sleep. It is the simplest napping behavior. You engage in preventive napping when you nap because you are tired. Even napaphobics occasionally engage in preventive napping when they have a significant amount of sleep loss—perhaps due to extensive work, partying, or mental fatigue. (Of course napaphobics will try to cover up their napping behavior.) Even the most unsophisticated napper can engage in preventive or replacement napping.

Preparatory Napping or Going to the Sleep Bank

Prophylactic napping behavior (or what I prefer to call preparatory napping) is reserved for the more planful napper. Preparatory napping anticipates future sleep loss. When nappers realize they may be in for an extended period of wakefulness, they will wisely engage in preparatory napping in order to enhance their performance hours later. Research suggests that naps can enhance performance anywhere from one to twelve hours after the nap. Expert nappers participate in preparatory napping before late nights, difficult work assignments, and stressful events. Preparatory napping is a more sophisticated level of nap behavior than preventive napping. Preparatory napping requires a napper who can think clearly about his or her napping behavior.

Pleasurable Napping or Simply Liking to Nap

Pleasurable or appetitive napping occurs because one simply has a desire to nap. Pleasurable napping can occur even though the napper is not tired. Many nappers consider pleasurable napping the highest order of napping behavior. When people engage in pleasurable napping, they are simply doing something they *like*. Pleasurable napping feels good—similar to the feeling one might get from a three-mile jog or a piece of chocolate cake. Unlike jogging or eating, however, pleasurable napping does not stress your joints or your waistline!

The Cost-Effectiveness of Napping

In summary, scientists have re-discovered a behavior that is normal, makes you feel good and act better, and can help overcome fatigue. Nappers of course, have known this for years. And the napping community has known for a long time what nonapapologists and the scientific community have not yet mentioned—*napping is cost effective*. In an era of shrinking household budgets and government cost overruns, one of napping's major advantages seems all too obvious—napping doesn't cost a cent. Science, logic, common sense, and cost arguments all coincide. One must wonder—why isn't everyone striving to become a better napper, and to be proud of it!

You must sleep sometime between lunch and dinner, and no halfway measures. Take off your clothes and get into bed. That's what I always do. Don't think you will be doing less

*work because you sleep during the day. That's a foolish
notion held by people who have no imagination. You will be
able to accomplish more. You get two days in one—well, at
least one and a half, I'm sure. When the war started, I had
to sleep during the day because that was the only way I
could cope with my responsibilities.*

—Winston Churchill,
quoted by Walter Graebner
in *My Dear Mister Churchill*

NAPPING PRIDE:
ON BECOMING A NAPPER

Winston Churchill was a proud napper. Indeed, if there were
a poster boy of napping (and there probably should be), Winston Churchill would be my nominee. He believed in napping
and he let people know it.

During a vacation to Jamaica I was able to visit the beach
where Mr. Churchill painted and napped. It was a cherished

highlight of my vacation. To be at the place where a famous napper napped is an unparalleled experience. Unfortunately, I was not allowed by the beach owners to nap on that beach. But I can still fantasize about that scene before I drift off into one of my own naps.

Napaphobic Influences

Unlike Winston Churchill our society does not encourage people to become proud nappers. In contrast, napaphobics in our society try to inflict their own their own fears of napping onto others. When they "catch" a person napping they wake that person up! Having committed *that* crime, they then try to make the person feel ashamed for napping. Is it any wonder that so many people remain closet nappers (or as I refer to them— *clappers*).

Many more people nap than talk about it. This lack of nap talk appears to be due to the influences of napaphobic individuals. Napaphobics can be so disparaging toward nappers that nappers become guilty about rather than proud of their own napping behavior.

Making Nappers into Clappers

Our nappist society has conspired in other ways to make what should be proud nappers into mere clappers. The workplace is notorious for inhibiting naps, even though naps could improve work performance and mood. Workers have to "sneak" their naps, and napaphobic colleagues try to "catch" them napping. Clappers closet themselves away—figuratively or literally—in order to engage in what should be considered healthy, normal, work-enhancing behavior. Clappers nap behind closed office doors, computer screens, books, and newspapers to escape being harassed by their napaphobic colleagues.

The Workplace as a Nap-place

A colleague of mine puts a sign on his closed office door which says, "Meditating—please do not disturb." I have suggested that he change the sign to read, "Napping—please do not disturb." The large chair in which he allegedly meditates is perfect for napping. I tried it!

In refreshing contrast to my colleague's clapping behavior is my wife Camille's napping behavior. After lunch she often goes into her boss's office when the boss is at a meeting. She naps on the boss's couch with the door open. Her colleagues have provided her with a light blanket for her afternoon naps. I couldn't be more proud of my wife! As you will see chapter 6, I have even named a nap after her.

Discrimination Exists Even in the Nonapapologists' Workplace

Even scientists who study napping behavior have had to deal with the prejudices of our nappist society. Nonapapologists have reported that early studies of sleeping behavior did not investigate napping behavior. That is, if the sleep did not occur at night, it was irrelevant to a sleep study! Furthermore, sleep studies often prohibited napping during the course of the study. What a double standard that was! In addition, explanatory models designed to explain human sleep ignored napping behavior. Even sleep researchers discriminated against napping!

The Predicament of the Napnoozler

Our nappist society has made *napnoozlers* out of many people. By napnoozler I mean someone who is forced to lie and deceive people about his or her napping behavior. I once met a woman who could not admit to others that she engaged in napping behavior. If someone telephoned her and woke her from an afternoon nap, she would say in her groggy voice, "Oh no, I wasn't napping." If someone sees a napnoozler napping, upon awakening the napnoozler will say, "I was just resting my eyes." Indeed "resting my eyes" is the mantra of napnoozlers—it is almost a biological marker for napnoozling.

Napnoozlers Are Not Napaphobics

A napnoozler, unlike a napaphobic, does not have a disorder that he or she attempts to inflict on other members of society. Napnoozlers are simply not yet strong enough to become proud nappers. Napaphobics, on the other hand, directly attempt to inflict their own nappist fears on other members of society. Indeed, napaphobics have made napnoozlers out of far too many of us. To create napping pride, compassionate nappers must vigorously combat the influence of napaphobics on our society.

Nap Talk

There are a number of ways nappers can help to change our nappist society. First of all, we need to be vigilant about nappist vocabulary, often used none-too-subtly by napaphobics. Proud nappers must inhibit people from using such phrases as *stealing* a nap, *sneaking* a nap, *going down* for a nap, and *caught napping*. Nappers *have* naps. They don't take, steal, or sneak naps. Nappers don't *go down* for a nap, they *prepare* for a nap. Nappers are never caught napping, because there is no crime to catch. Nappers are merely *seen* napping.

Napping Euphemisms

So-called euphemisms concerning napping must no longer be tolerated. Terms such as "resting my eyes" or "meditating" discourage napping pride. Indeed, there should be no such thing as a napping euphemism because there is nothing even mildly offensive about napping. As a matter of fact the term "napping euphemism" is itself an oxymoron. Society might need euphemisms for death and disease, but we certainly don't need euphemisms for something as positive, productive, and healthy as napping!

Knowing Your Napping Facts and Myths

Nappers must regularly confront napaphobics with the science of nonapapology. Napaphobics attempt to create more napnoozlers and fellow napaphobics by embarrassing nappers. With science on the side of nappers, however, we must turn the tables on napaphobics and embarrass them about their scientific ignorance. As already shown in chapter 2, science is not on the side of napaphobics but at the bedside of nappers.

While it may be impossible to change napaphobics' lack of napping behavior, it may be possible to quiet them down and restrict their influence on society in general. Their ignorance of the facts and myths of napping must be constantly exposed. Chapter 6 provides an entire glossary of napping words. *The Art of Napping* prepares you to intimidate obstinate napaphobics with both the science and the vocabulary of napping.

Knowing about Famous Nappers

In addition to scientific knowledge, dissemination of knowledge about famous nappers will also help to make our society more nap friendly. As more people learn about the benefits of napping from reading about Churchill, Edison, Da Vinci, Brahms, and other contemporary greats, more questions will be raised about society's customs and traditions about napping .

Society could do well by understanding the napping techniques and napping highlights of well-known figures. Our contemporaries who are famous must come out of the closet about their own napping behavior.

Famous successful people nap—and our nappist society must be helped to acknowledge that fact. As new books are written about them and about famous historical figures, we must insist that reliable napping information is included. This essential part of famous people's behavior is too often missing from written accounts of their otherwise interesting lives.

Proud Napping Begins at Home

Proud napping, however, undoubtedly begins in the family. I recently asked my teenaged daughter and three of her high school friends about their last nap. My daughter proudly cited her last nap at her friend's house. I of course complimented her for her success.

One of her friends, however, said she can not nap no matter how hard she tries. Another friend indicated that she prefers not to nap because she might miss something. The third friend was very vague about her ability and desire to nap.

I would imagine that none of my daughter's friends live in homes that encourage napping pride. I know their families encourage moral, ethical behavior—but they have probably neglected to include napping in that category.

The Family that Naps Together . . .

In contrast to the families of my daughter's friends, our family comes from a long line of nappers. Napping behavior has always been encouraged. We support one another's napping behavior. When we gather for large family vacations, for example, our family pays close attention to each member's napping skills. The living room of my parents' house has three couches (would you expect less!). The house also offers five bedrooms, soft chairs, comfortable rugs, and a sand beach just a hundred feet away. At any one time you might find five members of our family napping.

Napping Competition

On some days we might see how many naps a person can take in a twenty-four-hour period. Friendly napping contests are encouraged. I might awaken from my second nap of the day, only to look across at an adjacent couch where my cousin Denny is on his third of that same day—a fact reported in respectful awe by his children.

At times like these, you must simply tip your cap to the better napper and realize that on any particular day one napper can beat another. When a person is on a napping roll it is very difficult to compete with them. What's comforting to know is that your day will come, too, when on that day you might be the master napper of the family.

Napping Degree of Difficulty

Another way our family recognizes outstanding nap behavior is to rate one another's naps—in terms of degree of difficulty, much as you might rate the difficulty of a diver's dive or a skater's routine.

For example, if you nap while music is being played loudly, kids are jumping on your back, and you are five feet from a wild card game, your napping degree of difficulty is rated extremely high. Upon awakening you will no doubt receive many compliments from your admiring family. While you were napping, family

THE ART OF NAPPING

members would no doubt have been commenting proudly on your napping ability. (Interestingly, no one would remove the kids, turn the music down, or quiet the card game. Such a change in activity might disturb the napper, as will be discussed in chapter 4.)

Naps on the other end of the degree of difficulty are often discounted. Napping in the house while everyone else is at the beach (or vice versa), for example, rates a low level of difficulty and receives few to no compliments among seasoned nappers.

Napping Commentary

Naps which are rated somewhere in the middle of the degree of difficulty create much discussion. Are babies screaming in the same room as difficult to nap through as having older children sitting on your back? If you nap right after your spouse has asked you to go to the store (and you haven't yet), is that psychologically more difficult than napping right after you ask your kids to cut the lawn (and they didn't)? Or, how about the degree of napping difficulty for the kid who naps instead of cuts the lawn? If a father lies down to nap with his toddler, who has a greater degree of nap difficulty—the toddler or the father?

Discussions about degree of napping difficulty can often occupy much of the time between naps. The conversation at moments like these often leads people into reminiscing about one's easiest or most difficult naps. What could be more relaxing!

Becoming a Napping Judge

Just as a figure-skating judge knows whether a double axel is more difficult than a double salchow, a napping judge can make equally fine discriminations of difficulty. With practice you can rate your own naps and those of others.

Napping judges focus on how disquieting the environment is to the napper's senses. What are the levels of noise, light, temperature, and smell? Particularly important are factors affecting the sense of touch. How comfortable is the napping platform? Are people present who might interrupt the nap? Does the nap environment change during the course of the nap? By taking such variables into account, you can begin judging nap difficulty on a 1–10 scale.

I recently attained my highest napping score—during outpatient surgery under a local anesthetic. While the surgeons were beginning to sew what they estimated would be dozens of stitches, I told them I would be taking a nap. I was partially reclined in the surgeon's chair; operating lights were glaring in my eyes; members of the operating team were conversing

jovially; each stitch tugged slightly on my face; medicinal odors permeated the room. As I awoke from my nap, a nurse said softly to someone entering the room, "Be quiet, he's napping." After the operation was over, all present agreed it was a very, very impressive demonstration of napping prowess. Displaying no false modesty, I rate this nap a perfect 10!

A National Day of Napping

As more children are raised in a napping culture, our nappist society will begin to change. Perhaps we will have a National Nap Day. I would nominate the Friday after Thanksgiving as a leading candidate for National Nap Day. On this day some people might need a preventive nap after extensive holiday traveling or shopping. Other people might need a preparatory nap because they will be staying up late that night with their guests. Still others, having satisfied their appetite for eating on the day before, may wish to have a nap to satisfy their appetite for napping. Thanksgiving Friday could become our National Day of Napping.

Diagnosing Napping Difficulties

As society becomes more napper friendly, we must also work to help individuals (especially clappers and napnoozlers) who are not yet proud nappers. You can diagnose these traits by these individuals' unfortunate use of napping euphemisms and their response to some simple napping interview questions.

For example, ask if they would be comfortable knowing that the pilots of their airplane would be napping at different times during the flight. Do they quickly say something like, "What a good idea!" or do they have either a delayed response or a negative response? Ask them in front of their friends if they like to nap. Observe their reactions: Do they stammer, blush, or otherwise look uncomfortable? When you are speaking about your own personal napping highlights, do they say things like, "Oh I could never do that"? (In contrast, a napaphobic would try to make you feel guilty or silly about even discussing your napping prowess.)

Changing a Nap Attitude

Having identified people who nap but carefully hide their naps from others (clappers) or try to deceive themselves and others about their napping (napnoozlers) it is up to nappers to help them change their attitude. The first issue for them is not one of napping strategies (to be discussed in the next chapter) but first and foremost a problem of napping attitude.

This lack of commitment to napping can be overcome in

several ways. One way is to have them read *The Art of Napping*—especially chapter 2 on the science of napping and chapter 5 on famous nappers. You might also encourage them to discuss napping with proud nappers. They could be encouraged to set simple napping goals such as "I will take one nap this week and talk about it with a napper." In addition they might need to discuss certain elements of napping—like sleep inertia and/or different types of naps—with knowledgeable nappers.

Developing a Nattitude

Clappers and napnoozlers are alike in that they have some capacity to nap but need to improve their attitude about napping (i.e., develop a nattitude). In the next chapter various napping strategies and techniques are discussed. Engaging clappers and napnoozlers in conversations about napping techniques can also make them more comfortable about the concept of napping itself. With a little knowledge, the encouragement and support of friendly nappers, and a basic understanding of nap technique, more and more individuals can become proud nappers.

Napping is not simply "passing out" or "conking out," just as fine dining is not the same as fast food. Your napping style reflects your own individuality.

Nap Power

Proud nappers beget more proud nappers, and more proud nappers will change our nappist society. Proud nappers will openly discuss the virtues of napping; more and more magazine articles will appear on napping, and the subtly derogatory articles of napaphobics will disappear. Articles on the "Secrets of Staying Awake" which discuss the "willpower" it takes to stay awake will be replaced by articles on the "Secrets of Napping." These more enlightened articles will talk not about willpower, but nap power; not about the alleged benefits of forcing oneself to stay awake, but of the luxury of falling asleep.

z   z   z

Jim Lehrer of public television's "NewsHour" closes his office door every day at 12:30 P.M. for an hour's nap, while an assistant holds all calls. Even special correspondent Roger Mudd can't get through; he once left a message for Mr. Lehrer saying, "When snookums wakes up, have him call me."
—*Wall Street Journal*, June 26, 1995

NAP MANAGEMENT: GETTING THE MOST OUT OF YOUR NAP

Proud nappers who have some flexibility in their daily schedule can make sure that they have the opportunity to nap. Jim Lehrer started napping years ago while recovering from a heart attack. In comments that exude napping pride, Lehrer says, "If people have a problem with it, then to hell with 'em. It's the only good habit I ever developed in my life, and it's the best excuse I've found for avoiding a power lunch." While not wishing to minimize Jim Lehrer's many other accomplishments, I personally think this is the best advice he has ever given!

Napping without Shame

Proud nappers manage to seize napping opportunities in places or in ways that clappers and napnoozlers would find too embarrassing.

According to the Wall Street Journal, Nancy Tompkins, a San Francisco lawyer, simply lies down under her desk. "My feet stick out like the Wicked Witch of the East. The last time someone came in, he was so frightened he ran right out." In typical proud-napper language, Ms. Tompkins says, "Everybody I know wants to nap after lunch. If you're a hard worker, there's no reason you shouldn't do it with impunity."

Like Lehrer and Tompkins, more and more people are beginning to manage their naps by letting their associates know that one simply doesn't ask for them during certain periods in the afternoon because they are "unavailable."

Napping Style

To get the most out of your nap, you need to develop a napping style. While napping style is unique to each individual, there are three parts of the napping process around which one can style. The first part involves getting ready for napping. The napper must make sure the needed napping aids are present and that the environment is as nap friendly as is possible. The second part is the nap itself—or nap revelry. The final part of the napping process is après napping. Awakening from a nap may need the same attention that getting ready for the nap does. Experienced nappers know that to get the very most from their naps they must warm up and also cool down from the nap itself.

Getting Ready

Getting ready to nap is, for many people, the beginning of napping pleasure. The very act of "getting ready" can be almost as much fun as the nap. When we were toddlers there was usually a routine to getting ready to nap. Typical getting-ready activities might include drinking some juice, having one's diaper changed, getting out a favorite blankey, putting a stuffed animal in the crib, using a pacifier, and so on.

Just thinking about that time—when getting ready to nap was an important activity in one's day—arouses warm memories in proud nappers. And making a routine out of getting ready to nap can work for adults as well: turning on the TV or radio, beginning to read a book or the newspaper, changing into sweats, fluffing the pillow, taking off shoes, brushing teeth, etc. Doing activities like these in a particular sequence can replicate one's early experience of a napping routine.

For some people, eating lunch is considered part of the

getting-ready-to-nap routine. As a matter of fact, I know some people who consider the entire day between waking up in the morning and napping in the afternoon as part of getting ready to nap!

Napnomic Devices

Napnomic devices are aids that assist in napping. Each napper needs to discover their own napnomic devices. When a napper is getting ready to nap they look for their napnomics. Examples of common napnomic devices might be a book, magazine, newspaper, TV, radio, or a hammock.

Napnomic devices are as numerous and as common as the grains of sands on a beach (which in itself is a great napnomic). A cool breeze through the window, a drawn window shade, the warm sun, the sound of waves—these can be wonderful napnomics. Riding in a car can be wonderfully napnomic, as long as you are not the driver. Perhaps the most expensive napnomic device is an airplane. An airplane to an adult is like a crib to a toddler. When the flight attendant hands me my pillow and blankey I wonder—can the teddy bear be far behind?

Once I received a number of napnomic devices from my cousin for Christmas. What did he give me to keep all my napnomics in, you might ask? A napsack, of course.

Napping Revelry

Little needs to be said about the napping period itself. During the nap one simply *revels*. Nap reveling means that the napper takes great delight in the nap.

Nap revelry is enhanced if the nap environment stays constant from the beginning of the nap period to the end. In other words, if the environment is quiet at the start of the nap it helps if it is quiet during the whole nap—and likewise for a noisy environment. Remember, a toddler often wakes up when the noise from the car stops. If the environment starts to cool down during the nap period, having a person available to cover up the napper is helpful.

Nappers have compared nap reveling to the experience of cooling off in a mountain stream on a hot day, taking off one's ski boots after skiing, the first bite of one's favorite desert, or sinking into a hot bath.

Good nap reveling is most apt to occur when one does not have to worry about *nappus interruptus*. Nappus interruptus occurs when some one or some thing awakens a napper in mid-nap. Worries about nappus interruptus can impair napping performance. Nappers must make sure that any loved ones in the napping vicinity know not to wake the napper except in extreme emergencies. Minimizing the threat of nappus interruptus maximizes the benefits of the nap.

Après Napping

Just as après skiing is an important part of the skiing experience, après napping can be an important part of the total napping experience. Nappers who can take time after napping to stretch, walk, and/or shower can double their pleasure. Staying in the napping position—whether it be sitting, reclining, or lying down—for several minutes after one awakens can also be helpful.

For many nappers après napping is a no brainer—you just feel good immediately after awakening. However, for those individuals who from time to time experience sleep inertia, après napping can be improved. First of all, simply knowing that sleep inertia can happen and that it disappears within fifteen minutes is helpful. Avoid extremely difficult tasks for at least fifteen minutes after the nap ends. Also, schedule a pleasant task to do right after awakening. This could be meeting with a colleague, or reading an article or part of a book that is particularly appealing. Some people might use a good book, music, or a TV show to help them fall asleep and also to help them wake up. To further reduce the possibility of sleep inertia, one should nap before one is totally exhausted.

Immediately after a pleasurable activity a person often feels tired. So might a napper after a fine nap. But in both instances, one can be quickly refreshed.

Napping at Work

The process of napping is the same at work or at play. Because nappism is alive and well in our society, the work environment rather than the play environment is the more difficult of the two in which to nap. A proud napper who has an office can simply close the door and put out a sign indicating that he or she is napping. Better yet would be the workplace that simply closes down work for a period of time—a feat of business re-engineering that is still waiting to happen in North America. Until then, we must learn how to hide our napping from our colleagues while they are hiding their napping from us!

A CPA I know likes to nap while pretending to read the paper. A friend who manages mutual funds naps while appearing to talk on the phone. A teaching colleague places his hands in a praying position in front of his eyes and tries to look like he is in deep thought.

Once nappism diminishes somewhat, workers will be able to share their workplace napping strategies more openly. Until then, share *The Art of Napping* with co-workers and swap napping strategies with the enlightened among us.

A Nap-unfriendly Work Environment

When a skilled napper is getting ready to nap, he or she pays particular attention to the environment—which can facilitate or hinder the nap. In a work environment, for example, your unique napnomic devices may not be readily available. Time for après napping activities may not be possible. The nap environment may be difficult to control.

As technology advances into the workplace, the nap friendliness of the work environment is in retreat. The office cubicle, created by five-foot-high partitions on all sides, is one of our most difficult napping environments. Beginning nappers can't easily position themselves to nap discretely when people can see into their office from all sides. Fluorescent lights, windowless offices, computer screens, and the like can make napping more difficult.

While expert nappers can generally overcome a napnomic-less, hostile environment, novice nappers are at a significant disadvantage in many work environments. A nap-friendly technology and work atmosphere needs to be created in order for more workers to reach their potential. Fitness centers at the work site were created to enhance worker productivity—how about a napnasium in every business?

Napping at College

College is one huge napping opportunity. For the first time in their lives, many young people are living away from their parents. They must read a lot of books, listen to innumerable lectures, go to a library, often stay up too late—and, most importantly, one's desk is no more than twenty feet from one's bed! There is a plethora of napnomics at one's disposal. How could a person go to college and not nap?

College is also a place to test out one's napping relationships. I first napped in front of my future wife at college. I napped at the library while she studied, and not once did she complain about my napping. The only difficult place to nap at college is in small classes and seminars. Nappers plan their course schedules appropriately—no back-to-back small classes—and they make sure they schedule time for napping during some afternoons. I suspect that more students learn to nap at college than learn how to study.

Napping at Play

In our recreational activities we have become more comfortable with the idea of public napping. Go to a concert, a play, a baseball game, or the beach and observe for yourself—*people are napping*. Visit the wave pool area at a water park: The majority of people are not there to watch waves or the people in them, they are napping in one of the few places at a water park that has chaise lounges. More people's heads are nodding in the lounges than are bobbing in the waves.

Hikers and backpackers are beginning to admit that part of the joy of their sport is outdoor napping. People who are fishing or hunting are often napping as well (a fact that is no doubt comforting to the fish and animals); some have been known to fall to the ground or into the water as a result of their nap indulgence. People not only nap while boating, I have a friend who *loves* to nap in his boat while it is tied to the dock.

Napping—the Preferred Recreational Activity

Certain recreational activities are growing in popularity because they facilitate napping. How else could people spend three hours watching golf on TV other than for the fact that people nap while watching? At outdoor concerts on lawns, be especially careful not to step on a napper. I suspect yoga classes are more fashionable now because at the end of many classes people are given the opportunity to relax in a horizontal position—and they nap.

Public napping is truly becoming a major recreational activity—and is probably more popular than watching pro football. If pollsters would just include napping in their surveys of preferred recreational activities, napping would be rated the most popular way to recreate—hands or heads down! Of course the survey questions would have to be administered anonymously so that clappers and napnoozlers could answer honestly.

Advanced Nap Planning

Skilled nappers plan naps into their daily work and play schedules just like planning to attend a church or school meeting. Particularly when preparing for a late-night social event, they know that planning what to wear is less important than planning where and when to nap.

People who are going to a play or concert must plan whether to nap before or during the event, for example, and select their seats accordingly. Out of deference to the actors' feelings, my wife tries not to sit in the front row of our local community theater if she has not napped that afternoon. Her inevitable napping during a part of the performance is not a refection on the acting; rather it is a reflection on her poor nap planning on that day.

Expert nappers plan their next nap while taking their current nap. Winston Churchill arranged his work day around his nap schedule. Just as people take advantage of photo opportunities, nappers take advantage of napping opportunities. Amusement parks that have signs for amateur photographers indicating that this spot is a photo opportunity need to do likewise for inexperienced nappers.

They could place "napping opportunity" signs on particularly comfortable benches, lush lawns, certain sedentary rides, and quiet out-of-the-way sections of the park.

Synchronized Napping

Perhaps the highest level of advanced nap planning is called for by synchronized napping. Synchronized napping is especially important when a group or family wishes to do critical activities other than napping. In order for the group members all to go to an activity together, they must plan the activity and their naps so that no one's nap is interrupted.

Synchronized napping is similar to synchronized swimming in that the nap activities of the group must be choreographed. The group needs to know who is napping when, where, and for how long. The bottom line of synchronized napping is that for the period of time during which the social activity occurs, no one will have planned a nap and everyone who has wished to nap will have done so.

If group members just take their naps without being choreographed, the group will simply cease to function as a group. I have seen families and groups become dysfunctional when their naps are random rather than synchronized. On the other hand, a group that naps in a synchronized manner also interacts smoothly in many other areas of group functioning. A family or group that naps harmoniously will also play and socialize harmoniously. Not only are their members well rested, but they demonstrate an enviable understanding of their fellow group members' basic human needs.

z z z

Ronald Reagan, our fortieth president, elevated the nap to a high art form. Indeed, as nap enthusiast James Gorman once quipped, "Ronald Reagan was hardly ever awake!"
Not only did Reagan get plenty of rest in the White House, he also took some of the shame out of napping. Reagan was so comfortable with the habit that he often joked about it. Once, after sleeping through an incident in Libya, for example, he instructed his staff to wake him immediately "if anything important happens anywhere in the world—even if I'm in a Cabinet meeting."

—HR Focus, March, 1995

Famous Nappers: Profiles in Napping

No matter what one may think of President Reagan's politics, proud nappers applaud his napping style. In his inimitable way, he became the napping leader of the Free World. Could the Russian leadership match his napping ability? How disconcerting for America's enemies to know that their major adversary could nap independently of what chicanery they were up to. Perhaps we have not given napping its proper credit for hastening the fall of communism!

Reagan is but one of many famous nappers. Many napping anecdotes (napidotes) have been recounted about famous people. Perhaps some are apocryphal. But regardless of their authenticity, napidotes are part of our napping folklore, which proud nappers must take to their hearts as well as their beds.

Presidential Napping

World leadership and napping are inextricably linked. Presidents Coolidge, Kennedy, Johnson, Reagan, and Clinton, among others, all napped during their presidency. As already mentioned, Prime Minister Winston Churchill could be the poster boy of napping. President Kennedy, like President Reagan, left directions for people to awaken him from his nap only in instances of dire emergency. As told by Pierre Salinger, President Kennedy retired to a forty-five-minute nap immediately after lunch. He was able to go to sleep immediately and "was not to be disturbed during this rest except for reasons of high emergency."

It is obvious that presidents are serious about their napping. Clinton's presidency has displayed notable napping talent. According to various newspaper reports, Clinton can sleep in cars, trains, buses, and planes. While at home at the White House, he often naps from ten to thirty minutes. Sleep inertia does not seem to be a problem for Clinton: His aides say he wakes up quickly and totally refreshed.

Napping Generals

Picture a general napping near the battlefield. Is this not the ultimate power nap? Generals as disparate as Nap-oleon Bonaparte and Stonewall Jackson napped during battles.

Biographer Vincent Cronin states that Bonaparte could sleep at will—even when the guns were firing a few yards away. Bonaparte's biographer believes this ability to nap reveals much about Napoleon's personality. Cronin felt it showed Napoleon was "in harmony with his own deepest instincts and with the people around him." To me, napping ability is not a Rorschach ink-blot test—

it simply shows that Napoleon knew how to take care of himself! Too bad all the soldiers on both sides were not also napping; then there would have been a lot less killing.

Emperor Charlemagne took a mid-day nap that lasted about three hours. While we don't know if Charlemagne was proud of his napping, his biographers apparently were not. Coren in his book *Sleep Thieves* says that most every historian followed their reports of Charlemagne's nap prowess with an apology implying that Charlemagne was merely making up for lost sleep—an interpretation that tells more about the historians' napping attitudes than it does about Charlemagne. Perhaps Charlemagne napped because he liked to nap.

Napping Artists

If music and museums can cause one to nap, it logically follows (at least to me) that composers and artists themselves nap. It has been written that Brahms took seven years to compose his famous lullaby because he kept falling asleep at the piano. How great that must have been for Brahms!

I have heard the napidote that Salvador Dali napped with a spoon in his hand. When he was completely asleep, the spoon dropped to the floor and awakened him—an interesting nap management strategy.

Da Vinci is the artist whose napping behavior is most talked about. The napidote goes that Da Vinci would sleep in short fifteen-minute nap periods every four hours, thus sleeping a total of only one and one half hours per day! As a result he had many more hours during the day to do his creative work. Other people have tried to replicate Da Vinci's napping schedule with varying levels of success.

If the story about Da Vinci's nap management is true, it is an amazing napidote.

Regardless, stories about famous napping artists do reinforce the fact that creativity and napping are very compatible. As we shall soon see, creative ideas do occur while one is napping.

Napping Scientists

Not only is there a napping science, there are also napping scientists. No doubt the most famous napping scientist is Thomas Edison, who as the inventor of the electric light bulb is credited with creating our modern sleep-deprived society. In the personal diary he kept while on a vacation, Edison writes about his delight in napping; he enjoys recounting his napping dreams, and he uses metaphor for his expertise in being able to sleep "as sound as a bug in a barrel of morphine."

Edison, however, was a complicated man—even in his attitude toward sleep and napping. He tended to be a napnoozler, a clapper, and a napaphobic all wrapped up into one. For example, as a napaphobic Edison railed against the uselessness of "unproductive sleep." He gloried in the fact that the light bulb allows people to be "productive" for longer periods of time each day. Too much sleep, he stated, makes people unhealthy and in-efficient. While his words seem to personify napaphobia, his behavior indicates otherwise. A biographer of Edison, Robert Conet, quotes an Edison associate who remarked that Edison's "genius for sleep equaled his genius for invention. He could go to sleep anywhere, anytime, on anything." Such praise could serve as many a proud napper's epitaph.

Edison was a closet napper (clap-per) both figuratively and literally. Often he tried to hide his propensity for napping. On one occasion his as-sistant actually stumbled over him as

THE ART OF NAPPING

Edison napped in a closet. In addition, as a napnoozler Edison tried to foster the legend that he needed very little sleep. His biographer indicates that in reality Edison's braggadocio about not needing much sleep was a smoke screen to divert attention from his habit of frequent napping. One of Edison's scientific colleagues remarked that while Edison might have only four hours of sleep at night, he had two three-hour naps each day.

Once when Henry Ford stopped by Edison's lab, one of Edison's assistants stopped Ford from entering Edison's office because Edison was taking a nap. Ford was amused and remarked that he didn't think Edison slept that much. The assistant agreed: "He doesn't sleep very much at all, he just naps a lot." For all Edison's attempts to hide his napping behavior from the public, one of my favorite pictures of him shows him taking a nap on his laboratory table.

A Most Famous Nap

The story of the most famous nap in all of science is known tangentially by many scientists. While some scientists remain skeptical about its authenticity, it is in fact a true napidote.

One evening in 1865, a professor of chemistry named Friedrich August Kekulé began to nap in front of the fireplace. While he was napping he dreamed what some consider to be the most important dream in history. He dreamed of snakes (Freud would not be surprised!) twisting and turning. In Kekulé's own words, "One of the snakes seized hold of its own tail, and the form whirled mockingly before my eyes. As if by a flash of lightning I awoke . . . ."

This dream gave Kekulé the clue to a discovery which has

THE ART OF NAPPING

been called the cornerstone of modern science. Most simply it proposed that the molecules of certain organic compounds are not open structures but closed chains or rings—like the snake biting its own tail. We non-chemists can not fully appreciate the enormity of this discovery and its influence on all organic chemistry from that date forward. But as nappers we know, as did Kekulé, that very good things can happen when you nap.

Famous Napping Places

Most of us will not become famous nappers. We can be part of napping's greatness, however, by napping in famous places. We can nap where great people nap. Or if the crowd is large enough, we can nap in the presence of great people!

George Washington slept in many places. I would like to know where he napped. As napping becomes more popular, we might have tourist attractions advertised for the fact that "George Washington napped here."

You might attend a theater or use the same restaurant where a favorite famous napper once napped. All presidential libraries should have plaques or other commemorative displays showing how and where the president napped. As mentioned earlier, biographers of famous people will have to do a better job of describing the napping habits of their subjects. This will help other nappers visit the favorite napping sites and reflect on the nap strategies of famous nappers.

My Favorite Famous Napping Place

I get to go to my favorite famous napping place once a year. Each summer my wife and I and two other couples visit Tanglewood, Massachusetts, in the Berkshire Mountains to listen to the Boston Symphony perform at open rehearsals. Tanglewood advertises the opportunity to picnic on the lawn during and after the late morning rehearsals. I estimate that at least twenty-five percent of the people also nap on the lawn without any encouragement from the concert sponsors.

And it is a beautiful site—a potpourri of napping styles. Young and old on their backs, fronts, or sides, knees bent or straight-legged, eyes shielded by sunglasses or uncovered, napping individually, as couples, or in a group. Music and summer mountain breezes waft over the nappers as they relax in a panoply of shades of green grass and blue sky. It is a spectacular sight emblazoned into my napping memory.

On one particular day I returned to our picnic site to find my wife and four friends all napping simultaneously. It was a veritable napping full house—two kings and three queens. My eyes closed with pride as I settled in next to them, making six very satisfied concert-goers. Famous or not, everyone should have a favorite napping place.

Your Napping Community

The community of nappers is larger than it seems. Besides your friends, family, and colleagues who nap, you are part of an international napping community that includes not only presidents, generals, emperors, artists, and scientists but also Hollywood celebrities! Actress Sharon Stone, for example, says she restores her energy by taking a ten-minute nap before going out. For napnomic devices she uses eyeshades and a relaxation tape.

Nappers without a community are like a single fire ant. When a single napper's fondness for napping is criticized, he or she individually can't make much of a ruckus. But like fire ants, if a group of nappers is present when an individual's napping behavior is criticized, there will be repercussions. Famous and less-than-famous nappers have much in common and are all part of the napping family.

As more and more famous people go public about their napping, the napping community will display greater self-esteem. When asked about napping, you can confidently and honestly answer: "Yes, I nap, as a lot of famous people do." You know you are in good company when you are a napper.

Ilsa, She-wolf of the Napstopo

What's in a name? That which we call a rose
By any other name would smell as sweet.
                    —*Romeo and Juliet*, Shakespeare

Dictionaries are like watches; the worst is better than
none, and the best cannot be expected to go quite true.
                                        —Samuel Johnson

A NAPPING DICTIONARY:
THE VOCABULARY OF NAPPING

Based on the quotes above, you might wonder about the utility
of a napping dictionary. Why bother to spell out the meaning
of various napping terms? As Shakespeare would no doubt
attest, napping and nap-related activities are the same no matter
what you call them: "A nap by any other name would feel as
good." And if a lexicographer with the enormous stature of
Johnson believes that dictionary terms are never quite accurate,
why bother with a napping dictionary?

A Napping Dictionary Rationale

Mastering the vocabulary of napping is important for several reasons. First, it will help nappers talk to one another. Members of the napping community can use a napping language to make them feel special—much like the strange handshakes and traditional greetings that are exchanged by members of exclusive clubs. Second, special napping language can be used to intimidate obstinate or inveterate napaphobics. Nappers can communicate in words that only they know, and can use this language in such a manner that napaphobics feel left out—which is a perfect prescription for sedating the know-it-all attitudes of napaphobics. Third, a napping vocabulary can help society become less nappist. When a group (such as nappers) develops its own special culture of which members are proud, soon more and more people want in to that culture. In the blink of an eye (no pun intended), napnoozlers and clappers will want to belong openly to the napping community.

A Nalphabetical Dictionary

A dictionary of napping words is not arranged alphabetically. Rather, it is arranged *nalphabetically*. What this means is that the words are sequenced so that the first to be defined are those which may be used to explain later words. A napping dictionary is made to be read from the first word to the last.

It is expected that reading a napping dictionary will have the same effect as if you were reading a regular dictionary. You should get sleepy and want to nap. The napping dictionary practices what it preaches. Take a relaxing breath and turn the page. If you have been reading without your napnomics close at hand, this may be a good time to get them.

There ought to be a word for . . .

Naptitude—what you develop by reading and practicing *The Art Of Napping;* an aptitude for napping; a trait commonly found in leaders, geniuses, and babies.

Nattitude—another trait you develop by reading and practicing *The Art of Napping;* a proud attitude about your napping.

Nappeth—what God does to rest; also descriptive of short sleeps taken by Biblical characters.

Napping platform—a constructed device which is used for napping, and which may or may not have been designed with that purpose in mind (for example, a bed, couch, carpet, desk, boat, or concert seat).

Napnomic devices—activities, persons, things, or places that assist a person to nap. For example, talking (activity) to a mother-in-law (person) on the phone (thing) while on the couch (place) helps some people nap.

Napsack—a bag in which to carry napnomic devices.

Some Napping Transportation Terms Defined

Airplane—world's most expensive napnomic device; an environment in which you are not awakened from your nap and asked if you want something to eat; a place where strangers nap close together.

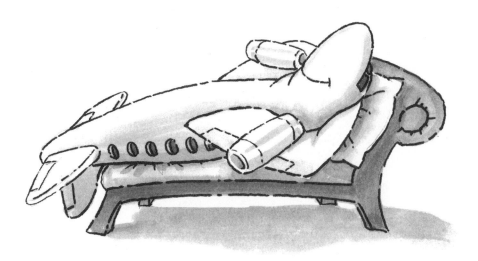

Nap attendant—a flight attendant whose main job is to help people nap so that they won't be a bother during the flight. (Not to be confused with a "nap assistant," who helps to maintain a constant environment—noise level, temperature, etc.—for one's naps.)

Autopilot—a napping pilot; as a group, pilots seem to be among the best nappers in the country, but the traveling public prefers not to know this fact.

Napmobile—a napnomic device especially designed for getting toddlers to nap while driving aimlessly and anxiously around the block; a device that also assists adults (preferably not the driver) to nap while traveling great distances.

Defining Your Napping P's and Q's

Definitions of the different purposes of napping needs to become basic knowledge to all nappers. Getting to know your napping P's and Q's is essentially a Napping 101 course—a course most college students master during their first semester.

1. **Preventive napping**—designed to ward off sleep deprivation; the simplest of all naps; a nap that you take because you are tired.

2. **Preparatory napping**—designed to anticipate sleep loss; often taken prior to a late night out to ensure effective functioning at a later time.

3. **Pleasurable napping**—a nap taken because napping feels good; sometimes called appetitive napping.

4. **Quintessential napping**—a nap which combines all three previous naps; a nap you take when you feel tired, when you anticipate feeling more tired, and also to quench your appetite for napping.

Types of Naps Defined

Following are some examples of naponyms, that is, naps named after some person, activity, or thing from which a given nap takes its name. Proud nappers will undoubtedly create their own naponyms. Name some after yourself or after your favorite people or activities. Here are some of my favorites:

Churchillian nap—a nap of epic proportions, taken in bed and without clothes on.

Biblical nap—a nap taken approximately every seven days or once a week, often on Sundays; also the nap you might take during a clergy's sermon.

Camille nap—most brazen of all naps, in which napper shows no concern for judgment of others as to one's napping behavior; you will recognize this nap when you see it; named for my wife.

Bill nap—a twenty-minute horizontal nap from which the napper easily awakens by him or herself in exactly twenty minutes; my favorite type of nap, and I did want to name a nap after myself!

Working nap—a nap taken while simultaneously problem solving, child rearing, or engaging in other types of vocational activity.

Brahms nap—a nap taken at the work site, just as Brahms is said to have napped at his work site—the piano; a nap which thankfully is becoming increasingly more popular with workers and, hopefully, with their employers.

Grampa Bill nap—a series of brief naps taken in a seated position and occurring intermittently throughout the evening, often in front of the TV; or the ultimate, contented nap taken by grandparents whenever they please as their ongoing reward for a life well lived.

Terminal nap—a euphemism for you-know-what; that great final nap.

Napping Diagnostic Terms

Napaphobic—a person with a deep-seated fear of napping; a person who attempts to inflict his or her disorder on other members of society; a person who tries to make nappers feel guilty and ashamed of their napping.

Napnoozler—a person who is a wannabe proud napper but who deceives people about the importance of napping in his or her life.

Clapper—a person who hides their napping from others; a person who is in the closet about their napping, either figuratively or literally.

Nappism—a characteristic of a society which practices discriminatory behavior and holds prejudicial attitudes against nappers and napping.

Napression—a condition of napaphobics in which the afflicted person attempts to cover up his or her latent desire to nap.

Napnostic—a nonbeliever in the healing power of naps.

Naphomaniac—a napper who overdoes a good thing.

Sleep inertia—an uncomfortable feeling of disorientation or confusion which sometimes occurs upon awakening from a nap; a normal feeling that disappears usually within fifteen minutes.

Nappus interruptus—an interrupted nap due to some person or thing awakening the napper; the pleasurable sensations of napping are abruptly halted—leaving the napper unfulfilled.

Naparcisstic—a conceited napper who needs counseling.

Constinaption—unable to nap for several days; napping irregularity.

More Napping Dictionary Terms

Home movies or videos—napnomic devices that help families and friends to nap simultaneously.

Snapper—a person who nags or snaps at a napper; often to blame for *nappus interruptus.*

Meditation—a euphemism for napping sometimes used by clappers and napnoozlers.

Napkin—a napper's relatives.

Napteria—the place where you call for a pre-nap meal.

Daynapper—a calendar with the time period of 2 to 5 P.M. shaded to indicate the time in which nappers might wish to schedule their naps.

Napestry—textile wall hangings that commemorate great or historically significant naps or nappers.

Nap police—people who restrict opportunities for napping; dressed in civilian clothes but acting as if nappers were criminals for being "caught napping."

Napstopo—the most dedicated nap police. *See page 62*

Sabbatical—paid excuse for a year of extra napping opportunities.

Telenapping—increased opportunities for napping as more people work at home or out of the office; napping in one's car or one's home during the work day.

Yoga—a series of mysterious body positions done prior to the main purpose of the session, which is to get horizontal and nap; a ritualistic, esoteric, napnomic activity.

MRI—an expensive napping platform which allows napping while obtaining a medical diagnosis; has been known to freak out non-nappers who don't see the MRI test as a napping opportunity.

College—an expensive setting where young people go to hone the napping skills they first learned as infants; rivals the beach as a preferred napping environment.

Napidote—napping anecdotes; may be apocryphal but authenticity is not their point anyway.

Napnasium—a place in which there are napping platforms where people can practice their napping.

Napercise—what one does in a napnasium.

Napperobics—nap training in which you vigorously practice your own napping routine; often conducted in a napnasium.

Step napperobics—nap training done by varying the height of the napping platform; will probably not catch on.

Naptivism—Intelligent, tasteful, and often witty activity of calling attention to one or more benefits of napping. Often conducted by napping publicly with great composure amidst chaos created by people who claim to need very little sleep.

Congratulations

You've done it! You've read an entire dictionary, maybe all in one sitting or all in one lying-down. But I doubt it. While this chapter will help nappers to create a new napping language, nappers must also continue to debunk society's pretentious language about napping. As pointed out earlier, nappers don't steal, take, or sneak naps; nor do nappers ever get caught napping. The language of napping is ever expanding. As you discuss napping with your fellow nappers, you will create new napping terms. How big can our dictionary get? In creating a dictionary of napping we are also inventing a new napnomic device! What an amazing field! Our language of napping will carry us with more self-awareness into the twenty-first century— the era of the nap.

Perhaps someday society will act to do something about
sleepiness. It may even come to pass that someday the person
who drives or goes to work while sleepy will be viewed as being
as reprehensible, dangerous, or even criminally negligent as the
person who drives or goes to work while drunk. If so, perhaps
the rest of us can all sleep a little bit more soundly.

—Stanley Coren, *Sleep Thieves*

A Look Ahead:
The Future of Napping

The future as painted by Coren seems a bit harsh. Hopefully, sleepiness will not be perceived as criminal. But it should be perceived as correctable. There is an alternative to constantly feeling sleep-deprived.

It just may be a fact of modern life that many people can't get enough sleep at night. They work long hours, attend meetings in the evening, and get up at night with young kids. Their mornings start too early because they need to get the kids out the door for school on time, do work around the house before going to their other work, etc. No matter what the reason, many people just can't get enough sleep at night.

Fortunately, there is an alternative to sleep deprivation—and nappers know what it is. Whether you are a morning person or a night person, getting up early or staying up late, you can always be a nap person.

A National Sleep Debt

We hear constant talk about various countries' financial debt. Yet there is another type of debt which countries are experiencing, and that is the sleep debt of their citizens.

Analyses of the cost of sleepiness in the United States are astounding. Sleep researchers have estimated that errors and accidents due to sleepiness cost the United States around fifty-six *billion* dollars per year! Worse yet, thousands of deaths and millions of disabling injuries result from accidents related to sleepiness. Survey data indicate that one in five adults surveyed has showed up late for work or missed work entirely because they didn't sleep well the night before. And it is now almost folklore that the Exxon *Valdez* tragedy, which cost ten billion dollars, would not have occurred if the third mate, who was at the wheel of the ship at the time of the disaster, had taken a nap on the evening that he was on duty.

The congressionally created National Commission on Sleep Disorders Research has disseminated so many statistics on sleep deprivation that we get sleepy reading them. It is a penchant for governmentally created bodies to focus on our problems rather than our solutions. Perhaps we need a National Council on Napping to look into the obvious way to solve our sleep debt.

The Consequences of Sleep Loss

Most studies of sleep behavior collect data in the laboratory. The most intriguing study I have read about, however, collected data from events in the real world, not the laboratory.

Stanley Coren analyzed 1.5 million Canadian traffic accidents that occurred in 1991 and 1992—looking specifically at the Monday just after daylight savings time began in the spring and the Monday just after daylight savings time ended in the fall. He found that immediately following the spring switch to daylight savings time, when everyone had just lost one hour of sleep, there was a seven percent *increase* in traffic accidents. In the fall, when everyone gained one hour of sleep, there was an immediate seven percent *drop* in accidents. Amazingly, after just one hour of sleep loss for everybody there are seven percent more traffic accidents, and the reverse is true if people gain an extra hour of sleep.

Think of the accidents and errors, other than traffic accidents, that are also occurring on that day but for which national statistics are not kept. Perhaps the Sunday after daylight savings time begins should be a recommended nap day. As a public service, newspapers should remind people that in addition to turning their clocks forward on Sunday they should also nap. How about: "Turn your clocks forward an hour at around 2 A.M. and your sheets down for at least an hour around 2 P.M."

The Cost Effectiveness of Napping

A poll conducted by The Better Sleep Council (I do like that name!), as reported in *Entrepreneur* magazine, found that a full third of the one thousand adults they surveyed admitted that sleeplessness had affected their job performance. Can you imagine the collective gnashing of teeth that would have occurred if the pollsters had found this same lack of worker productivity due to alcohol?

To reverse the decline in worker productivity due to sleep loss, we need some nap counseling at the workplace—a task for which we don't need professional counselors, just the opportunity to talk openly about napping strategies with our co-workers. Yet until now business consultants have missed the importance of workplace napping. New office technologies seem to have re-engineered napping out of rather than into the workplace. We have consultants trumpeting the one-minute this and the five-minute that. But what we don't have is the obvious solution to worker productivity—the thirty-minute nap.

A Myriad of Napping Advantages

Increased productivity and the resulting cost benefits are obvious advantages of napping. Just think of all the other advantages.

You can't eat or smoke while you're napping. After an intensive napping period, there is no need to shower. Most people don't need special clothes or expensive equipment to nap. Napping can make your stress go away—at least for the time you are napping. Napping is a natural medicine. Could "a nap a day keep the doctor away"? Or how about, "Take two naps and call me in the morning."

Napping recasts what many people view as a problem—that is, sleep deprivation—into a ready-made solution. People are not "sleep deprived"; we are simply "nap ready" —ready to treat ourselves to the only no-cost, no-sweat way to physical and emotional health.

THE ART OF NAPPING

New Places to Nap

As the many advantages of napping become better known, more people will be seen napping in more places. Have you ever visited somebody's house and thought to yourself—their couch, their porch, their yard, what great places to nap they would be? I would love to have an invitation such as, "Why don't you come over for dinner and take a nap on the porch before we eat?"

Places where people are already napping need to be more encouraging of nap behavior. Airports must be more accommodating to nappers—perhaps there should be a napnasium in every airport. Public parks can put out "napping opportunity" signs to highlight the very best places to nap. Rest stops on interstate highways can be renamed correctly as nap stops.

Automobile technology has been very lax in figuring out ways to help people nap in their cars. Reclining seats are simply not enough. Footrests, pop-up pillows, easy storage for blankets, and so on need to be part of the option package. How about a way to convert the back seat and the trunk into a bed?

In essence, more and more people are looking to nap. Private companies and public services have to advertise that they have thought of the napper. Nappers are going to be a major market force.

Future Nap-Friendly Technology

So many of our past technological accomplishments have hindered the development of napping behavior. Bright fluorescent lights, jet engines, and conveyor belts, for example, are simply not nap-friendly innovations. But there are nap-friendly developments on the horizon. There is already a place to talk about napping on the Internet. You can now share napidotes in cyberspace.

No doubt the most nap-friendly technology, however, consists of current and future innovations in the computer industry which allow even more people to work at home. Worker productivity will increase not because more people are working on computers, but because more people will be napping when and where they very well please. You are more apt to get up early and work, and/or work late at night, if you know you can nap at your leisure!

The Work Environment of the Future

Only a few companies allow napping at the workplace. Fewer still have any policies around napping. Policies and procedures around napping are probably not what is needed. Workers don't need to be told how, when, or whether to nap. A policy which simply recognizes the relationship between lost productivity and sleepy workers, with a suggestion that napping at work is okay, should be sufficient.

Nap breaks as well as coffee breaks can become a part of the workplace culture. Perhaps in the future workers will drink a natural, nap-inducing liquid rather than nap-inhibiting coffee. Napping seminars will be offered to workers. Similar to the How to Study courses that college students often take, workers (and those few college students that need it) will take a course in How to Nap. An interesting development for the workplace is the file-a-bed mentioned earlier, which is a desk with a fold-up bed in it. Just as you sit at your desk and work, you can now lie down at your desk and nap. As far as I'm concerned, the desk/bed is an innovation whose time has come.

THE ART OF NAPPING

Napping While You Work

Napping at work is coming. Napping *while* working is coming, too. Numerous nappers (both famous and not so famous) have recounted how they developed solutions to problems or came up with new insights while asleep. The napidote about the scientist Kekulé is no doubt the most famous. But many of us ordinary nappers have "napped on a problem."

When stuck on how to organize a particular chapter or page in *The Art of Napping,* I did what you would expect of me—I napped on it. (Maybe that's why I took six years to write this book?) The print shop manager who made copies for me of each chapter said he could probably nap while he was making copies of *The Art of Napping.* I told him that would be the ultimate compliment.

The problem with napping while working is that it doesn't look like work to most people, and unfortunately often to the boss. Yet we know that while we are napping our brain is working. While our sensations are somewhat diminished during a nap, our senses of sight, touch, and hearing are still active. Obviously if napping while working is going to be encouraged, a major effort to educate the uninformed needs to occur.

Sometime in the not too distant future, when we are struggling with a problem, our enlightened bosses will suggest: "Have you tried napping?"

Parenting While You Nap

Most every parent can relate to the fact that they are working while they nap. To a new parent the opportunity to nap is like winning the lottery—it really doesn't get any better than having the time to nap. Yet parents are still working while they are napping. In particular they are listening selectively.

A parent can nap through the often ear-splitting sounds of children playing, but the whimper of an infant or the sound of one's child in trouble awakens the napper instantly. Thus, a parent can be working hard at listening selectively while enjoying the nap. A problem with parenting while you nap may occur if one of the parents is napaphobic and doesn't understand that what looks to him or her like a spouse "napping on the job" is really "doing the job while napping."

Napping parents must not be embarrassed when asked about their napping. Rather they must explain calmly to their spouses that they were having a "working nap." Parents, like everyone else, can work and nap at the same time.

A Napping-While-Working Napidote

I have been told the napidote of a Nobel Prize winning scientist who served as a consultant to a particular laboratory. As part of his consultation, he would listen to a series of project briefings from the lab's scientists. During presentations made to him, his habit was to periodically say "Ya" and vigorously nod his head affirmatively. This behavior was meant to encourage people to continue, to show his understanding of their explanation, and/or to confirm the direction their science was taking them. The briefings lasted all day, and as the day lengthened the head nodding would become less vigorous; his eyes would close for long periods of time, and the "Ya" response disappeared entirely.

The senior lab scientists expected this to occur, and first-time presenters in particular were directed to simply continue their presentation, including the visual aids. What amazed all the scientists in attendance was that if a presentation went in a direction that the consultant did not find useful and/or seemed illogical, he would awaken and vigorously say "No." The consultant seemed to be napping and listening simultaneously! As one of the scientists who recounted this napidote to me remarked, "It was as if he could nap through good physics, but not bad physics."

Progress in Napping

In the past six years that I have been thinking about writing *The Art of Napping*, I have been observing people's napping behavior. The number of people napping publicly seems to be increasing. As the world realizes that napping is a preferred activity of many people, basic nap etiquette should begin to improve. Competition for the napper's dollar is just starting.

I have been observing airplane nappers, for example, who are customers of the very competitive airline industry. It is interesting to note that flight attendants try not to wake their on-board nappers. They allow you to miss their food rather than your nap. I for one appreciate such mature and thoughtful nap etiquette. Other industries and settings will no doubt follow the lead of the airlines. The twenty-first century may well become an epic napping epoch.

Good day, good re-reading, and good napping.

z   z   z